SAINT
GEORGE
Patron Saint of England

Lois Rock
Illustrated by Finola Stack

LION
CHILDREN'S

Who Was George?

George has been respected as a saint for nearly 1,700 years. From long ago, Christians believed that George was buried at a place called Lydda, in Roman Palestine. Pilgrims went there to honour George and to pray to God.

One story is that George was a Christian in Lydda who gave his money to the poor and began telling people all about Jesus. At the time, it was against the law of the Roman empire to be a Christian, so the Roman ruler of the town had him put to death.

But soon amazing stories were being told about him. Some said that George had been chopped into pieces... but God had brought him back to life. He had been buried deep in the earth... but God had brought him back to life. He had been thrown into a blazing fire... but God had kept him safe.

It is little wonder that, around the year 495, the leader of the church, the pope, gave a warning: he said that George was one of the saints who deserved respect, but his true deeds were known only to God!

Even so, Saint George remained very popular. Churches were built in his honour and the stories about him were told by pilgrims in many different places. He was probably well known in England by the eighth century; indeed, one book of Saint George stories was translated into Anglo-Saxon!

This stained-glass picture of Saint George shows him killing a fierce dragon.

George:
A Soldier for England

The tales about George always described him as a soldier. As a result, soldiers going to battle had special respect for him. In 1098, there was a famous battle at a place called Antioch. European armies were on a Crusade to capture the holy lands from the Saracens. A story arose that Saint George had appeared to them and helped them win.

Some years later, an English king, Richard the Lionheart, (reigned 1189–99) was taking part in

A church built in the Holy Land by the Crusaders.

a Crusade, and a new story arose that Saint George appeared to encourage him. Some people think that Richard may have used the cross of Saint George to decorate his fighting equipment.

By the fourteenth century, Saint George's arms of a red cross on a white background were used as a kind of uniform for English soldiers and sailors.

The emblem of the Order of Saint George.

Around 1347 the English king, Edward III, founded an order of knights – the Knights of the Order of Saint George. It still exists today, although it is usually known as the Order of the Garter. A chapel linked to the order was built in Windsor Castle – the Chapel of Saint George.

The most famous story about Saint George tells of him slaying a dragon. Some people might think this story is just made up, and then go on to think that everything else about Saint George is made up too.

In fact, inventing stories about heroic deeds was once a way of showing respect to real people. It may also be a picture story – a way of explaining that the real George was not afraid to stand up for what he thought was right, no matter how great the danger, and that his bravery led other people to believe in Jesus.

Dragon-Slayer!

L ONG AGO, in the city of Selena, in Libya, the people lived in fear. A terrible dragon had made its home in the nearby marshes. Its stinking breath carried disease, and the only way to keep the dragon from doing even more harm was

to give it food to satisfy its hunger.

'We have plenty of sheep,' the people agreed. 'Each day, we shall drive two sheep off to the marshes. That should keep the dragon quiet.'

The plan worked. The dragon gobbled the sheep and lay waiting for the next day and the next meal.

This went on for a very long time. In the end, the people had no sheep left.

'What shall we do now?' the people asked their king.

The king shook his head sadly. 'I have been thinking of everything possible,' he said. 'It is not easy, but I fear we will have to sacrifice ourselves.' The people gasped. What did he mean?

'I hereby make a law,' said the king. 'Each day, we will send someone to be the dragon's victim. We will draw lots to find out who must go.'

So that was the law. The townsfolk wept as, one by one, they saw friends and neighbours walk to their deaths.

'I would rather die myself,' said an old grandmother, as she watched her grandson go. 'Why should I not be allowed to take his place?'

'That is what the king has ordered' sighed her friend,

holding her and trying to comfort her.

The following day, the lots were drawn again.
An official stepped forward to announce the result.

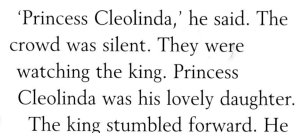

'Princess Cleolinda,' he said. The crowd was silent. They were watching the king. Princess Cleolinda was his lovely daughter.

The king stumbled forward. He was shaking. 'I cannot bear this,' he said. 'I will give you all my gold and silver if you let me keep my daughter.'

'What about my grandson?' shrieked the old lady. 'I wasn't allowed to save him!'

At this the whole crowd began shouting and shaking their fists. 'It's your law,' they shouted. 'We won't let you out of your own law! Send your daughter to the dragon, or we'll burn your house down and you with it!'

The king soon saw that he could not make them change their minds. But he had one more plea. 'Let me have her eight more days,' he begged.

12

The king spent the time hugging his daughter and weeping with her.

When, on the final day, he dressed his daughter like a bride, it was to lead her to the dragon's lair.

Princess Cleolinda cowered among the reeds, shaking with fear. A man came riding by – George, a soldier, with sword and spear.

'What's the matter?' he asked the girl. 'Why are you here in this wild place?'

'Oh, hurry away, sir!' she replied. 'A dragon lives in this place, and I have been sent to be its next victim, so it does not come and destroy the whole town.'

The soldier was a Christian, and he was dismayed. 'I will not allow it,' he said. 'In the name of Jesus Christ, I will help you.'

As they were talking, the dragon came running towards them. George drew his sword and made the sign of the cross of Jesus. Then he rode full tilt at the dragon and pierced him with his blade.

'Now, Princess,' cried George, 'untie your belt and tie it round the dragon's neck.'

Trembling, Cleolinda hurried to obey. Once she had done so, the dragon became as meek as a lamb, and she led it into the city, with George riding beside her.

As they approached the city, some people who were out in the fields saw the dragon.

'Help! Run! Save yourselves! Here comes the dragon!' they screamed. The panic spread like wildfire. As they reached one set of city gates, there were people running out of other gates, hoping to escape to the hills.

'Don't be afraid,' cried George. 'Instead, believe in God and Jesus Christ. If you will be baptized to declare yourselves Christians, then I will slay the dragon.'

The king had come hurrying to see his daughter. When he heard George's plea, he asked to be baptized at once. Then the townspeople all followed his example.

George took out his sword and sliced off the dragon's head. The town was saved.

'I shall build a church here in honour of God,' announced the king. 'I will also dedicate it to Mary, the mother of Jesus, and to George, who has saved us.'

At the place where the church was built, a fountain began to bubble up from between the rocks. Its pure water was good for drinking, and cured many who were sick.

'I will give you all the wealth you desire,' the king said to George.

'Do not give it me,' replied George. 'Instead, give your wealth to help the needy.

'Take care of the new churches in your kingdom.

Honour the priests who serve in them, and listen to their teaching. And always take care of the poor.' Then George said goodbye and left.

Saint George's Day

Saint George's Day began officially in England in 1222. A church council meeting in Oxford agreed that 23 April should be kept as a lesser holy day.

However, in 1415 an archbishop decided that it deserved more importance, and ordered it to be celebrated as much as Christmas!

Nowadays, it is again less important. It only gets mentioned in church services, and sometimes the flag is flown.

Today, Saint George is most remembered in England for the cross that he is said to have worn on his armour – red on a white background. It has become the English flag. At sporting events the flag is waved as a sign of national pride.

A church flying the English flag on Saint George's Day.

A Prayer Inspired by Saint George

Here is a prayer for Saint George's Day:

Dear God

We think about the story of Saint George,

a soldier who fought in the name of Christ.

We think about the story of Saint George,

who was concerned to help the poor and needy.

Help us to be brave, to fight

for what is right and to battle

for justice.

Index

Text by Lois Rock
Illustrations copyright © 2005 Finola Stack
This edition copyright © 2005 Lion Hudson

The moral rights of the author and illustrator
have been asserted

A Lion Children's Book
an imprint of
Lion Hudson plc
Mayfield House, 256 Banbury Road,
Oxford OX2 7DH, England
www.lionhudson.com
ISBN 0 7459 4810 3

First edition 2005
10 9 8 7 6 5 4 3 2 1 0

A catalogue record for this book is available
from the British Library

Typeset in 15/20 Revival565 BT
Printed and bound in Singapore

Picture Acknowledgments
Front cover: Sonia Halliday Photographs
Alamy Ltd: p. 6, 20
The Royal Collection © 2004, Her Majesty
Queen Elizabeth II, p. 7
Sonia Halliday Photographs: p. 5